TO THANK AND BLESS

TO THANK AND BLESS

PRAYERS AT MEALS

Second Edition

Dietrich Reinhart, O.S.B.
Michael Kwatera, O.S.B.

LITURGICAL PRESS
Collegeville, Minnesota

www.litpress.org

Cover design by Ann Blattner. The illustration on the cover is a roundel in Beuronese style added to a wall in the Saint John's Abbey refectory in 1995, as is the roundel at the head of the Easter Season I prayers in this book. The other roundels reproduced here were part of Br. Clement Frischauf, O.S.B.'s 1932 design for the Abbey refectory. Photos by Alan Reed, O.S.B.

1   2   3   4   5   6   7   8   9

Library of Congress Cataloging-in-Publication Data

Reinhart, Dietrich.
     To thank and bless : prayers at meals / Dietrich Reinhart, Michael Kwatera. — 2nd ed.
          p.   cm.
     ISBN-13: 978-0-8146-3170-6 (alk. paper)
     ISBN-10: 0-8146-3170-3 (alk. paper)
     1. Church year—Prayer-books and devotions—English.   2. Grace at meals—Christianity.   I. Kwatera, Michael.   II. Title.

BV30.R45 2007
242'.8—dc22

                                        2006006565

*Dedicated to our parents
in whose homes we first learned to pray at meals,
and to our monastic family at Saint John's Abbey,
who still teach and encourage us to pray.*

CONTENTS

FOREWORD

Good Italian patriarch that he was, Saint Benedict (c. 480–c. 547) knew that the dinner table is a sacred place for families to gather. That is why he included many helpful directions for community meals in his Rule for monks; for example, he insisted that everyone "come to table before the verse so that all may say the verse and pray and sit down at table together" (43:12, *RB 1980: The Rule of St. Benedict* [Collegeville: Liturgical Press, 1981] 245). Benedict knew that it isn't always easy to get the family rounded up before the food gets cold (even if they are hungry), and he believed that prayer should nourish the spirit before food nourishes the body.

Prayers before and after meals are part of the ancient tradition of Jewish and Christian worship that each generation of believers must make its own. They help dedicate the day to God just as morning and evening prayers do; indeed, busy families may find that meals provide the best (or only) opportunities for prayer together.

The prayers in this book were written a decade ago and, after falling on the ears of our brethren at Saint John's Abbey for a good long while, have been revised to reflect a deepening experience of the church's liturgical year. The heart of each season's prayers is a common introduction and response, drawn from Scripture, expressive of that season's central meaning and, thus, proclaimed from day to day. A variety of opening words, blessings and thanksgivings—based on Scripture as well—surround each season's core and disclose the richness hidden in these all too familiar words. Those who use these prayers will hear echoes of the Scripture readings proclaimed at the Sunday and weekday Eucharist and thereby continue to be formed by the Word of God.

In several prayers, the leader is invited to include the names of particular persons (those who prepared the meal, family members who are ill), but this might be done whenever the sense of the text encourages it. The inclusion of the names of loved ones will make these prayers more personal.

Blessings upon your table and upon all who taste there the Lord's spiritual and bodily nourishment!

Dietrich Reinhart, O.S.B.
Michael Kwatera, O.S.B.

June 1, 1983

PREFACE
to the Second Edition

After enjoying a welcome place alongside condiments and nap-kins, *Prayers at Meals* has been out of print for many years. Contin-ued requests for copies of this booklet have prompted us to prepare a second, expanded edition.

The Saint John's Abbey table prayers presented here had already undergone a revision with an eye to some simplifying of expression and to eliminating some masculine language for God. We have made a few similar changes for this edition.

Historically, the commitment to devoting a significant amount of time each day to liturgical and private prayer has whet the monastic appetite for variety in such prayer. Thus, a third set of prayers for Ordi-nary Time III has been added to celebrate the harvest season's gifts to our tables. Also, special prayers have been prepared for the solemnities and some feasts of the liturgical year. In this new section, prayers for the solemnity of the passing [death] of Saint Benedict (March 21) and for the feast of Benedict, Patriarch of Western Monasticism (July 11) have been included, especially for use in Benedictine monasteries.

As Saint John's Abbey celebrates its sesquicentennial during 2006–2007, we offer this revised edition of table prayers to gratefully commemorate 150 years of Benedictine prayer and work in central Minnesota. *In omnibus glorificetur Deus*—may God be glorified in all things.

Dietrich Reinhart, O.S.B.
Michael Kwatera, O.S.B.

June 24, 2006
Solemnity of the Birth of
Saint John the Baptist

Aptate vestras lampades

Trim your lamps.

ADVENT

*These prayers are used from the Saturday evening preceding
the First Sunday of Advent through Christmas Eve.
They could be included in the ceremony of
lighting the Advent wreath.*

PRAYER 1

Before the meal

Leader: Just as the rain and the snow
come down from heaven,
giving seed for sowing and bread to eat,
so shall the word be
that goes forth from the mouth of God.
A voice cries:
"Prepare in the wilderness a way for the Lord.
Clear a highway across the desert for our God."

All: Every valley shall be lifted up,
every mountain and hill brought low.

Leader: Sow freely, Lord God, the seed of your blessing
upon our table and upon all of us.
May it strengthen us to serve you
and each other,
through Jesus Christ, our Lord.

All: Amen.

After the meal

Leader: Lord our God,
we thank you for this meal together
and for inviting us to accept your reign
like children taking bread
from the hand of their parents.
Let us live in your peace,
at home with you all the days of our lives.
We ask this through Christ our Lord.

All: Amen.

PRAYER 2

Before the meal

Leader: The victory of the Lord is near,
already it is close,
the day of salvation shall not be delayed.
A voice cries:
"Prepare in the wilderness a way for the Lord.
Clear a highway across the desert for our God."

All: Every valley shall be lifted up,
every mountain and hill brought low.

Leader: All-powerful God,
look kindly on us,
bless this table,
and unite us to all people everywhere
who wait for the coming of your Son,
Jesus Christ, the Lord.

All: Amen.

After the meal

Leader: We thank you, Giver of all good gifts,
for the grace of life renewed,
the strength of life together,
and the promise of life to come.
We make this prayer through Christ our Lord.

All: Amen.

PRAYER 3

Before the meal

Leader: The Savior does not call out
or lift his voice high,
nor does he make himself heard
in the open streets.
But a voice comes before him saying:
"Prepare in the wilderness a way for the Lord.
Clear a highway across the desert for our God."

All: Every valley shall be lifted up,
every mountain and hill brought low.

Leader: Lord, bless the food we are about to eat
and bless the cooks *(name them)*
who have labored to prepare it.
Make us all a sign of the One
whose coming we await,
Jesus Christ, the Lord.

All: Amen.

After the meal

Leader: Give us grateful hearts, our Father,
for all your mercies,
and grant us the grace to love others
as fully as you have loved us
in Jesus Christ, our Lord.

All: Amen.

Before the meal

Leader: The Lord God is our refuge and strength,
a helper close at hand in times of distress.
A voice cries:
"Prepare in the wilderness a way for the Lord.
Clear a highway across the desert for our God."

All: Every valley shall be lifted up,
every mountain and hill brought low.

Leader: Lord God,
bless this table
and let the food we share
strengthen us in your service.
We ask this through the One
who comes in your name
and keeps us safe,
Jesus Christ, the Lord.

All: Amen.

After the meal

Leader: Ever-faithful God,
we thank you
for showing us your goodness
and loving-kindness at this meal.
We ask the same blessings
for all the members of your family,
through Jesus Christ, our Lord.

All: Amen.

Dne spes mea a ivventute

Lord, you are my hope from my youth.

CHRISTMAS

*These prayers are used from Christmas Day through
the Feast of the Baptism of the Lord. This section includes
a proper prayer for Christmas Day (December 25),
for the solemnity of Mary, Mother of God (January 1),
and for the Epiphany (Sunday between January 2 and January 8).*

December 25
CHRISTMAS DAY

Before the meal

Leader: Lord,
with angels and shepherds
we come in spirit to Bethlehem
and welcome our promised Savior, Christ the Lord.
Joyfully we name him:
Wonder-Counselor, Mighty-God,
Eternal-Father, Prince-of-Peace.

All: Unto us a child is born,
unto us a son is given. Alleluia!

Leader: God of glory,
bless this food we share as your family.
Show to all people,
especially those who lack enough to eat,
your goodness and loving-kindness.
We ask this through the One who is born to us,
Jesus Christ, our Lord.

All: Amen.

After the meal

Leader: Lord God,
we thank you for your nourishing gifts to us
on this festival day.
May the birth of your only-begotten Son
be a source of life for body, soul, and spirit.
Glory to you, O God,
in highest heaven and through all the earth,
both now and for ever.

All: Amen.

Before the meal

Leader: Lord,
you have made our gladness greater,
you have made our joy increase.
For you are called:
Wonder-Counselor, Mighty-God,
Eternal-Father, Prince-of-Peace.

All: Unto us a child is born,
unto us a son is given. Alleluia!

Leader: Lord our God,
bless this food we are about to eat
and look kindly
upon those who have prepared it:
(name them).

We ask this through your Son, Jesus,
who out of the wonder of your love
lives in our midst,
now and for ever.

All: Amen.

After the meal

Leader: We thank you, Lord God,
for the wonders you work—
for food and friendship in your house.
Above all,
we thank you for the gift of your Son,
who is one with us
both now and for ever.

All: Amen.

PRAYER 2

Before the meal

Leader: Dwellers in a land dark as death,
we have seen a great light.
The Lord in his radiance
shines upon us.
And this is the name we give him:
Wonder-Counselor, Mighty-God,
Eternal-Father, Prince-of-Peace.

All: Unto us a child is born,
unto us a son is given. Alleluia!

Leader: Mighty God,
visit this table
and renew the strength and vision of us all.
Bless your gifts and our time together,
through Jesus Christ, our Lord.

All: Amen.

After the meal

Leader: God of power and might,
we thank you for looking upon us in our need.
Help us bend our strength day by day
toward serving your people,
through Christ our Lord.

All: Amen.

Before the meal

Leader: O God, we ponder your love
within your house.
Your praise, like your name,
reaches the ends of the earth.
For you are called:
Wonder-Counselor, Mighty-God,
Eternal-Father, Prince-of-Peace.

All: Unto us a child is born,
unto us a son is given. Alleluia!

Leader: Eternal Father,
we praise and bless you
for the goodness you show us
at this meal and throughout this season.
Be with us as we celebrate
the fulfillment of your promise
in the coming of your Son,
Jesus Christ, our Lord.

All: Amen.

After the meal

Leader: Eternal Father,
accept our thanksgiving
for bringing us together
to share this meal.
Keep us as faithful witnesses
to the joy which is ours
in the gift of your Son,
Jesus Christ, the Lord.

All: Amen.

PRAYER 4

Before the meal

Leader: Hear what the Lord God says—
a voice speaking peace
for God's people and God's friends.
He is called:
Wonder-Counselor, Mighty-God,
Eternal-Father, Prince-of-Peace.

All: Unto us a child is born,
unto us a son is given. Alleluia!

Leader: God of harmony and peace,
bless us as we enjoy the gifts
you have given us.
May our eating together
be a sign of the peace and goodness
you give to all people
in your Son, Jesus Christ the Lord.

All: Amen.

After the meal

Leader: Lord Jesus, Prince of Peace,
may the blessings we share
strengthen us to bless others
with your Christmas gift of peace.
We give thanks to you,
to the Father and the Spirit,
both now and for ever.

All: Amen.

January 1
MARY, MOTHER OF GOD

Before the meal

Leader: God of glory,
all time and all the ages belong to your divine Son.
With the Blessed Virgin Mary
we rejoice to name him:
Wonder-Counselor, Mighty-God,
Eternal-Father, Prince-of-Peace.

All: Unto us a child is born,
unto us a son is given. Alleluia!

Leader: Eternal God,
we ask you to bless this food,
those who have prepared it,
and those who share it at this table.
Strengthen us to live as your people
in the new year that you give us.
We ask this through Jesus Christ, our Lord.

All: Amen.

After the meal

Leader: Praise to you, Giver of blessings,
for nourishing us at this festive meal
as we begin the new year.
In company with Mary,
who sang of your abundant gifts to the hungry,
we glorify you and give you thanks,
both now and for ever.

All: Amen.

Sunday between January 2 and January 8
EPIPHANY

Before the meal

Leader: Begotten before the world or time began,
the Lord of all is revealed this day
for our salvation.
With those of every nation,
we adore him and name him:
Wonder-Counselor, Mighty-God,
Eternal-Father, Prince-of-Peace.

All: Unto us a child is born,
unto us a son is given. Alleluia!

Leader: God of glory,
a blazing star made manifest
the mystery of your Word made flesh.
In his sacred name,
we ask you to bless this festive table,
and to make the brightness of your holiness
shine upon us,
both now and for ever.

All: Amen.

After the meal

Leader: Lord of all peoples,
we thank you for the abundant gifts
we have shared at this meal.
Grant that our lasting treasure
may be offering you humble praise
and giving generous service to others,
through Jesus Christ, our Lord.

All: Amen.

Lvcerna pedibus meis verbum tvvm

Your Word is a lamp for my feet.

ORDINARY TIME I

*These prayers are used during the weeks following
the Feast of the Baptism of the Lord until Ash Wednesday.*

PRAYER 1

Before the meal

Leader: Everlasting God,
Maker of the wide world,
you never grow weary
of those you have created.
Everything waits for you full of hope,
all the living ask you for food.

All: You open your hand, always in time,
and sustain our every moment.

Leader: Creator of all,
in your kindness, bless this food.
Give us strength
and bring us anew
to the task of building your kingdom.
We ask this through Christ our Lord.

All: Amen.

After the meal

Leader: We thank you, our Lord and Maker,
for the gift of food
and rejoice in the daily call to serve you.
To you be praise,
both now and for ever.

All: Amen.

PRAYER 2

Before the meal

Leader: Lord our God,
all is yours in heaven and on earth.
Everything waits for you full of hope,
all the living ask you for food.

All: You open your hand, always in time,
and sustain our every moment.

Leader: Lord,
bless our table
and make it a sign
of our belonging to you and to each other,
through Christ our Lord.

All: Amen.

After the meal

Leader: Lord,
we thank you for the bountiful love
you show to those who share our table
and to those dear to us,
through your Son, Jesus,
both now and for ever.

All: Amen.

PRAYER 3

Before the meal

Leader: Lord,
we commit ourselves to you,
trusting in your great love.
Everything waits for you full of hope,
all the living ask you for food.

All: You open your hand, always in time,
and sustain our every moment.

Leader: Lord,
bless our family through this meal
and renew the energies we use in your service.
We ask this in the name of Jesus Christ,
in whom all things hold together,
for ever and ever.

All: Amen.

After the meal

Leader: Father,
we thank you for this food
and all the daily reminders
of your care for us.
To you, Guardian of all,
be honor and glory,
both now and for ever.

All: Amen.

PRAYER 4

Before the meal

Leader: Lord,
the world around us comes from you,
and we praise you for this gift of love.
Everything waits for you full of hope,
all the living ask you for food.

All: You open your hand, always in time,
and sustain our every moment.

Leader: Lord,
bless this food
you have given us in your love.
Renew us in mind and body
as we share this meal,
through Christ our Lord.

All: Amen.

After the meal

Leader: Lord,
we thank you for the food
that strengthens us
and empowers us to share your gifts with others
as did your Son, Jesus,
who loves us
both now and for ever.

All: Amen.

Frvctvs arboris seduxit nos

The fruit of the tree led us astray.

LENT

*These prayers are used from
Ash Wednesday through noon on Holy Thursday.*

PRAYER 1

Before the meal

Leader: We have sinned against the Lord, our God,
and can only wait in prayer and fasting
for a time of favor.
Let us be confident.
Though our sins are like scarlet,
they shall be white as snow.

All: Though they are red as crimson,
they shall be made like wool.

Leader: God of our ancestors,
may our time of prayer and fasting
open us to your work of forgiveness
and free us to rejoice
in the saving work of your Son,
Jesus Christ, our Lord.

All: Amen.

After the meal

Leader: Lord God,
we wait for you to bring down our strongholds
and break the hold of sin in our lives.
We thank you
for nourishing us as we wait
and preparing us for the new life to come,
through Christ our Lord.

All: Amen.

Before the meal

Leader: We have stumbled in our sinful ways,
as if we could not be healed.
Let us return to the Lord, our God.
Though our sins are like scarlet,
they shall be white as snow.

All: Though they are red as crimson,
they shall be made like wool.

Leader: God of mercy,
uncover your face
and be gracious to us.
Heal us
and out of your own bounty
give us new life,
through Christ our Lord.

All: Amen.

After the meal

Leader: Merciful God,
we thank you for your kindness,
which exceeds all we ever knew of you.
To you, Healer of us all,
be honor and glory,
both now and for ever.

All: Amen.

PRAYER 3

Before the meal

Leader: Now is the time to lay down fear
and purify our love through serving others.
Though our sins are like scarlet,
they shall be white as snow.

All: Though they are red as crimson,
they shall be made like wool.

Leader: God, holy and strong,
bless this food
and give us strength
to bring your love
to those in suffering and pain
(especially _____).
We ask this through Christ our Lord.

All: Amen.

After the meal

Leader: We thank you, Lord, for calling us,
for nourishing us
that we might sacrifice ourselves.
To you, God of the poor and the lowly,
we pledge our strength,
both now and for ever.

All: Amen.

PRAYER 4

Before the meal

Leader: Let us turn back to the Lord, our God,
who is gracious and compassionate,
long-suffering and ever constant,
always ready to relent.
Though our sins are like scarlet,
they shall be white as snow.

All: Though they are red as crimson,
they shall be made like wool.

Leader: Ever-patient God,
meet us as we set ourselves to know you,
and leave a blessing upon our table
and all those dear to us.
We ask this through Christ our Lord.

All: Amen.

After the meal

Leader: Abiding Lord,
we thank you for this meal
and for your faithful presence in our lives.
As we grow more deeply open to you,
we shall praise and magnify your name,
for ever and ever.

All: Amen.

Filivs Dei redemit nos

The Son of God has redeemed us.

EASTER TRIDUUM

*The Easter Triduum is a three-day celebration of
the Lord's death and resurrection. It begins on Holy Thursday
"with the evening Mass of the Lord's Supper,
reaches its high point in the Easter Vigil,
and closes with evening prayer on Easter Sunday"*
(Roman Calendar, no. 19).

*The following prayers are used on the most holy days of
the Lord's passion, death, and resurrection.*

HOLY THURSDAY

Before the meal

Leader: Christ for our sake
became obedient unto death.
Let us worship him and say:
We adore you, O Christ, and we praise you.

All: Because by your holy cross
you have redeemed the world.

Leader: Lord Jesus,
be with us as we share this meal.
Prepare us to celebrate with faith
the saving deeds you have worked for us,
and let us share in your passing-over
from death to life,
both now and for ever.

All: Amen.

After the meal

Leader: Glory and praise to you, Lord Jesus Christ,
for sharing yourself with your apostles
at the Last supper
and for giving your love to us
at this meal.
Give us grateful hearts
for the life you poured out for us,
for the suffering that takes our sin away.
Glory and praise to you, Lord,
both now and for ever.

All: Amen.

GOOD FRIDAY

Before the meal

Leader: Christ for our sake
became obedient unto death,
even to death on a cross.
Let us worship him and say:
We adore you, O Christ, and we praise you.

All: Because by your holy cross
you have redeemed the world.

Leader: Lord Jesus,
it is right that we should glory in your cross,
for you bring us life, salvation, and resurrection.
Draw us closer to you at this table,
and let us share in your passing-over
from death to life,
both now and for ever.

All: Amen.

After the meal

Leader: Glory and praise to you, Lord Jesus Christ,
for dying on the cross
so that all might receive the life
that never ends.
Give us grateful hearts
for the life you poured out for us,
for the suffering that takes our sin away.
Glory and praise to you, Lord,
both now and for ever.

All: Amen.

HOLY SATURDAY

Before the meal

Leader: Christ for our sake
became obedient unto death
even to death on a cross.
Therefore God has exalted him
and given him the name above every name.
Let us worship him and say:
We adore you, O Christ, and we praise you.

All: Because by your holy cross
you have redeemed the world.

Leader: Lord Jesus, victor over death,
fill this time together with your blessing.
Remove the sadness that sin places in our hearts,
and let us share the joy of your passing-over
from death to life,
both now and for ever.

All: Amen.

After the meal

Leader: Glory and praise to you, Lord Jesus Christ,
for making holy the graves of all believers
and for giving joy to all who have died.
Give us grateful hearts
for the life you poured out for us,
for the suffering that takes our sin away.
Glory and praise to you, Lord,
both now and for ever.

All: Amen.

EASTER SUNDAY

Before the meal

Leader: God ever-faithful has guided our fasting
from food and sin,
and now bids us feast on abundant mercy
in the risen Christ.
Let us rejoice and be glad!
For behold, Jesus died
and now lives for evermore. Alleluia!

All: He has gone before us.
Yet he is with us for all time. Alleluia!

Leader: Giver of new life,
bless your gifts to us at this table.
Be present here as our guest,
until the day we join you
in the paschal feast of heaven,
for ever and ever.

All: Amen.

After the meal

Leader: We thank you, O God, on this most holy day
for gladdening our hearts at this festive meal.
With Peter and the apostles,
who ate and drank with the risen Lord,
we proclaim your goodness and love,
for ever and ever.

All: Amen.

EASTER SEASON I

*These prayers are used from
Easter Monday until the Ascension of the Lord.*

PRAYER 1

Before the meal

Leader: This is the day the Lord has made.
Let us rejoice and be glad,
let us praise the Lord for his goodness.
For behold, Jesus died
and now lives for evermore. Alleluia!

All: He has gone before us.
Yet he is with us for all time. Alleluia!

Leader: Lord,
(*during the Easter octave:* on this most holy day)
(in this most holy season)
let your blessing rest upon us
and upon our table.
Strengthen us in this time together.
We ask this in Jesus' name.

All: Amen.

After the meal

Leader: Blest are you, Lord our God,
who gather us together in Jesus' name.
We thank you for sharing your life with us,
both in this meal
and in all the ways you sustain us,
through Christ, our risen Lord.

All: Amen.

PRAYER 2

Before the meal

Leader: We have cause for abiding joy;
for God raised Jesus up
and set him free from the grip of death.
Behold, Jesus died
and now lives for evermore. Alleluia!

All: He has gone before us.
Yet he is with us for all time. Alleluia!

Leader: Father,
bless this food and this time together.
Strengthen us to live together in love,
united to Jesus,
whom you have made both Lord and Christ,
for ever and ever.

All: Amen.

After the meal

Leader: God of our joy,
we thank you for this meal
and for all that comes to us
through your beloved Son,
who is truly risen from the grave,
for ever and ever.

All: Amen.

PRAYER 3

Before the meal

Leader: The Father has given us birth
into a living hope
that nothing can destroy
or spoil or wither.
For behold, Jesus died
and now lives for evermore. Alleluia!

All: He has gone before us.
Yet he is with us for all time. Alleluia!

Leader: Ever-merciful God,
bless this table,
and nurture our faith
'til it grows into
praise, glory, and honor
at the revelation of Christ Jesus, our Lord.

All: Amen.

After the meal

Leader: Upholder of all,
we put our faith in you,
and offer our thanks for this meal.
Protect us by your power
until salvation is revealed
at the end of time
in Christ Jesus, our Lord.

All: Amen.

PRAYER 4

Before the meal

Leader: The Father, having found us in our brokenness,
has mercifully made us whole
in the body of his Son.
Behold, Jesus died
and now lives for evermore. Alleluia!

All: He has gone before us.
Yet he is with us for all time. Alleluia!

Leader: God who reconciles,
bless the food we are about to eat,
and let this meal together
be a sign of the unity
we share for all time
in the body of our risen Savior,
Jesus Christ, the Lord.

All: Amen.

After the meal

Leader: We thank you, the one Lord,
for nourishing this family
and molding us into a holy people.
United in Jesus Christ,
risen from the dead,
we give you praise
both now and for ever.

All: Amen.

Pignus futurae gloriae

Pledge of future glory

EASTER SEASON II

*These prayers are used from
the Ascension of the Lord through Pentecost Sunday.
This section includes proper prayers for
the Ascension and Pentecost.*

ASCENSION OF THE LORD

Before the meal

Leader: Blest are those who are called to feast
with the ascended Lord
and to celebrate his glorious triumph over death.
For behold, Jesus died
and now lives with the Father for evermore. Alleluia!

All: He has gone before us.
Yet he is with us for all time. Alleluia!

Leader: Lord Jesus,
send your blessing upon us and upon this food
as you sent it upon your disciples
at your ascension.
Raise us to new life with you,
here at this table and in your heavenly kingdom,
for ever and ever.

All: Amen.

After the meal

Leader: God of the heights and depths,
heaven is wedded to earth in your Son, Jesus Christ.
All thanksgiving be yours
for nourishing us with gifts for body and spirit,
through the same Christ our Lord.

All: Amen.

PRAYER 1

Before the meal

Leader: The Lord Jesus has not forsaken us.
He will come back,
glorious in the love of his Father.
For behold, Jesus died
and now lives with the Father for evermore. Alleluia!

All: He has gone before us.
Yet he is with us for all time. Alleluia!

Leader: Lord Jesus,
send your Spirit to bless this table.
Give us joy in knowing the love
in which we live and move
and have our being,
for ever and ever.

All: Amen.

After the meal

Leader: Lord Jesus,
because you live
we too have life in abundance
as we share this meal
and as we come to know the Father.
To you, Lord of all,
be honor and glory
both now and for ever.

All: Amen.

PRAYER 2

Before the meal

Leader: The Lord has ascended on high
and now our life
lies hidden with him in God.
Behold, Jesus died
and now lives with the Father for evermore.
Alleluia.

All: He has gone before us.
Yet he is with us for all time. Alleluia!

Leader: Lord Jesus,
the fullness of your love
fills the universe in all its parts.
Send your Spirit
to bless this table
and fill us with your life,
for ever and ever.

All: Amen.

After the meal

Leader: Lord Jesus,
true life of all,
we thank you for nourishing us
as we await the day
when you will come again.
Prepare us for the glory
which will be ours
in union with you,
for ever and ever.

All: Amen.

PRAYER 3

Before the meal

Leader: At last the God of glory dwells among us.
The old order has passed away.
For behold, Jesus died
and now lives with the Father for evermore. Alleluia!

All: He has gone before us.
Yet he is with us for all time. Alleluia!

Leader: Lord Jesus,
whose Spirit dwells within us,
be with us at this table.
Nourish us for the kingdom
where you are the First and the Last
and the living One,
for ever and ever.

All: Amen.

After the meal

Leader: You are blest, Lord Jesus,
in our thanksgiving for this meal
and blest is your holy name.
Through your Spirit
you make all things new.
To you belongs all time
and all the ages,
for ever and ever.

All: Amen.

PRAYER 4

Before the meal

Leader: We have been brought into one body
by baptism in the one Spirit,
and that one Holy Spirit
was poured out for us to drink.
Behold, Jesus died
and now lives with the Father for evermore. Alleluia!

All: He has gone before us.
Yet he is with us for all time. Alleluia!

Leader: Lord Jesus,
in your love, bless this table
and unite us more closely to you.
We make this prayer
gathered in your Spirit,
both now and for ever.

All: Amen.

After the meal

Leader: Lord God,
we thank you for this meal
and praise you for the gift of your Spirit,
who takes our life
and the inmost thoughts of our hearts
and transforms us
into the likeness of your Son, Jesus Christ,
who lives and reigns
for ever and ever.

All: Amen.

PENTECOST

Before the meal

Leader: How great is the mystery we celebrate:
the Spirit of the Father and the Son
gives us the paschal promise
of eternal life and joy.
For behold, Jesus died
and now lives with the Father for evermore. Alleluia!

All: He has gone before us.
Yet he is with us for all time. Alleluia!

Leader: Giver of all good gifts,
send your Spirit to bless the food and drink
at this table,
and grant that we may be nourished abundantly
with your presence.
We ask this through Christ our Lord.

All: Amen.

After the meal

Leader: We thank you, God of our joy,
for delighting us with the gifts
we have shared at this meal.
Through the power of your Holy Spirit,
make us the living proclamation of your Gospel:
"Jesus Christ is Lord."
Yours be the glory, for ever and ever.

All: Amen.

Lavs tva semper in ore meo

Your praise shall be ever in my mouth.

ORDINARY TIME II

*These prayers are used during the weeks following
Pentecost Sunday until September 1.*

PRAYER 1

Before the meal

Leader: Blessed is the Lord our God,
Creator of the universe,
who provides nourishing food
for all creatures
and sustains the whole world
with goodness, kindness, and loving favor.

All: Give thanks to the Lord, for he is good,
for his mercy endures for ever.

Leader: All merciful God,
send your life-giving Spirit
on our household
and on all dear to us,
and bless this table
as we join together and say:

All: Amen.

After the meal

Leader: Give us grateful hearts, our Father,
for all your mercies,
and make us mindful of the needs of others,
through Jesus Christ, our Lord.

All: Amen.

PRAYER 2

Before the meal

Leader: God calls us
to share in the life of the beloved Son,
Jesus Christ the Lord.
In this is our hope secured,
for Jesus lives to bring us
the Father's goodness, kindness, and loving favor.

All: Give thanks to the Lord, for he is good,
for his mercy endures for ever.

Leader: Ever-faithful God,
bless the food we are about to eat
and unite us in mind and heart
to your Son,
Jesus Christ, the Lord.

All: Amen.

After the meal

Leader: God our strength,
we thank you for food, life,
and the enduring hope
that you share with us
through Jesus Christ, our Lord.

All: Amen.

PRAYER 3

Before the meal

Leader: There is nothing in death or life,
nothing in all creation
that can separate us from the love of God
in Christ Jesus the Lord.
For to this day he sustains us
with his goodness, kindness, and loving favor.

All: Give thanks to the Lord, for he is good,
for his mercy endures for ever.

Leader: All-loving God,
bless this table
and through the work of your Spirit
shape us into the likeness of your Son,
Jesus Christ, the Lord.

All: Amen.

After the meal

Leader: Source, Guide, and Goal of all that is—
to you, Lord,
be praise and thanksgiving,
both now and for ever.

All: Amen.

PRAYER 4

Before the meal

Leader: How great is the hope to which God calls us,
how tremendous the power
available to us who trust in God!
For God's Holy Spirit abides with us
and fills us
with goodness, kindness, and loving favor.

All: Give thanks to the Lord, for he is good,
for his mercy endures for ever.

Leader: Great and generous God,
nourish us in this meal.
Strengthen our hidden selves,
that through faith
Christ may dwell in our hearts
in love,
both now and for ever.

All: Amen.

After the meal

Leader: Searcher of minds and hearts,
your power, working in us,
does infinitely more
than we dare to ask or imagine.
To you be glory and honor
in the Church
and in Christ Jesus,
for ever and ever.

All: Amen.

Ego svm vitis vos palmites

I am the vine, you are the branches.

ORDINARY TIME III

*These prayers are used from
September 1 until the First Sunday of Advent.*

PRAYER 1

Before the meal

Leader: The earth has yielded its fruit,
for you, our God,
have blessed us generously.
Abundance flows in your steps,
your open hand fills all our needs.
Great are your wonders,
God here among us,
God, our gladness.

All: Let the peoples praise you, O God;
let all the peoples praise you.

Leader: Lord of the harvest,
bless this food,
which comes to us in your gracious love.
Let your goodness be for us and all people
the source of abundant life and health,
both now and for ever.

All: Amen.

After the meal

Leader: Giver of all good gifts,
we thank you for the fruits of the earth
that we have shared in this meal.
As you have made our land
bear a rich harvest,
make our hearts fruitful
with the life and love of your Son,
Jesus Christ, our Lord.

All: Amen.

PRAYER 2

Before the meal

Leader: Master of seedtime and harvest,
rich is the feast your love provides:
nourishing food for body and spirit.
Great are your wonders,
God here among us,
God, our gladness.

All: Let the peoples praise you, O God;
let all the peoples praise you.

Leader: Bountiful God,
we ask you
to bless the food you have given us
and those who have prepared it: *(name them).*
Grace our table with your presence,
and grant us a place
at your banquet in heaven,
for ever and ever.

All: Amen.

After the meal

Leader: God, our Provider,
we thank you for the food
that strengthens us in your service.
May what we have sown by our labors today
produce an abundant harvest for eternity,
through Jesus Christ, the Lord.

All: Amen.

PRAYER 3

Before the meal

Leader: God of majesty,
you have filled the world
with light and life;
field and forest sing out your glory.
Great are your wonders,
God here among us,
God, our gladness.

All: Let the peoples praise you, O God;
let all the peoples praise you.

Leader: Lord, so glorious in holiness,
let your blessing rest on our table,
and let your favor abide
with those who cannot be with us.
Show to all people,
especially those who lack enough to eat,
your goodness and loving-kindness,
both now and forever.

All: Amen.

After the meal

Leader: Maker of all that is seen and unseen,
we gratefully acknowledge you
as the source of beauty and abundance.
As your gifts of nature refresh us in this life,
let your love bring us
to the joys of eternal life
with Jesus Christ, our Lord.

All: Amen.

PRAYER 4

Before the meal

Leader: Praise rightfully belongs to you,
Lord God,
for you crown the year with abundance;
in goodness you sustain our lives.
Great are your wonders,
God here among us,
God, our gladness.

All: Let the peoples praise you, O God;
let all the peoples praise you.

Leader: Source of all that is good,
bless us and these your gifts.
As we sit down together at this table,
draw us closer to you and to each other
in the bond of love,
both now and for ever.

All: Amen.

After the meal

Leader: We give you thanks, gracious God,
for multiplying your blessings among us
in Christ Jesus.
Give your saving help
to all peoples of the earth,
so that the poor and the needy
will acclaim you
as the source of their joy,
both now and for ever.

All: Amen.

PRAYER 5

Before the meal

Leader: From age to age you keep your promise,
O God our Savior:
as long as the earth lasts,
sowing and reaping proclaim your love.
Great are your wonders,
God here among us,
God, our gladness.

All: Let the peoples praise you, O God;
let all the peoples praise you.

Leader: Ruler of nature,
bless the food we are about to eat,
and bless those whose toil has produced it
for our enjoyment.
Let us see your gracious hand
in all your works,
so that we may rejoice in your goodness
all our days,
both now and for ever.

All: Amen.

After the meal

Leader: Hope of all the earth,
we thank you for making our land fruitful
and our table plentiful.
Grant that as we sow the works
of mercy and love,
we may reap the harvest of peace
in Christ Jesus,
both now and for ever.

All: Amen.

Before the meal

Leader: Lord our God,
all things, all times and seasons,
are of your making.
You spoke, and they came to be,
created by the breath of your mouth.
Great are your wonders,
God here among us,
God, our gladness.

All: Let the peoples praise you, O God;
let all the peoples praise you.

Leader: God, Provider of all,
send your blessing on our table
and on our house.
Strengthen us
through your plentiful gifts,
so that our joyful service may give you glory,
both now and for ever.

All: Amen.

After the meal

Leader: Creator of all that is,
receive our thanksgiving for this food
and for this time together.
Help us to live in harmony
with all of your creation,
so that we may guide it
to perfect fulfillment
on the day of Jesus Christ, the Lord.

All: Amen.

RESPONSE SHEETS

*The following pages of seasonal responses
may be duplicated for use by those at table.*

ADVENT

Verse by the Leader ends with:

> "Prepare in the wilderness a way for the Lord.
> Clear a highway across the desert for our God."

Response:

All: Every valley shall be lifted up,
every mountain and hill brought low.

*Prayer of Blessing to which **ALL** respond:*

AMEN.

CHRISTMAS

Verse by the Leader ends with:

> Wonder-Counselor, Mighty-God,
> Eternal-Father, Prince-of-Peace.

Response:

All: Unto us a child is born,
unto us a son is given. Alleluia!

*Prayer of Blessing to which **ALL** respond:*

AMEN.

ORDINARY TIME I

Verse by the Leader ends with:

> Everything waits for you full of hope,
> all the living ask you for food.

Response:

> **All:** You open your hand, always in time,
> and sustain our every moment.

*Prayer of Blessing to which **ALL** respond:*

> AMEN.

LENT

Verse by the Leader ends with:

> Though our sins are like scarlet,
> they shall be white as snow.

Response:

> **All:** Though they are red as crimson,
> they shall be made like wool.

*Prayer of Blessing to which **ALL** respond:*

> AMEN.

Easter Triduum
HOLY THURSDAY, GOOD FRIDAY, HOLY SATURDAY

Verse by the Leader ends with:

> We adore you, O Christ,
> and we praise you.

Response:

> **All:** Because by your holy cross
> you have redeemed the world.

*Prayer of Blessing to which **ALL** respond:*

> AMEN.

EASTER SEASON I

Verse by the Leader ends with:

> Behold, Jesus died
> and now lives for evermore. Alleluia!

Response:

> **All:** He has gone before us.
> Yet he is with us for all time. Alleluia!

*Prayer of Blessing to which **ALL** respond:*

> AMEN.

EASTER SEASON II

Verse by the Leader ends with:

> For behold, Jesus died
> and now lives with the Father
> for evermore. Alleluia!

Response:

> **All:** He has gone before us.
> Yet he is with us for all time. Alleluia!

*Prayer of Blessing to which **ALL** respond:*

> AMEN.

ORDINARY TIME II

Verse by the Leader ends with:

> . . . goodness, kindness,
> and loving favor.

Response:

> **All:** Give thanks to the Lord, for he is good,
> for his mercy endures for ever.

*Prayer of Blessing to which **ALL** respond:*

> AMEN.

ORDINARY TIME III

Verse by the Leader ends with:

> Great are your wonders,
> God here among us,
> God, our gladness.

Response:

> **All:** Let the peoples praise you, O God;
> let all the peoples praise you.

*Prayer of Blessing to which **ALL** respond:*

> AMEN.

Sicvt cedrvs Libani

Like a cedar of Lebanon

SOLEMNITIES AND FEASTS

These prayers are used on solemnities and several feasts throughout the year, arranged in chronological order. The response for each prayer matches the one used during the liturgical season in which the solemnity or feast occurs.

Saint Joseph. . . . . March 19

Passing of Saint Benedict, Father of Monks. . . . . March 21

Annunciation of the Lord. . . . . March 25

Most Holy Trinity. . . . . .Sunday after Pentecost

Most Holy Body and Blood of Christ . . Sunday after Trinity Sunday

Most Sacred Heart of Jesus. . . . . Friday after the
Body and Blood of Christ

Nativity of John the Baptist. . . . . .June 24

Saints Peter and Paul . . . . June 29

Benedict, Patriarch of Western Monasticism. . . . . .July 11

Assumption of the Blessed Virgin Mary. . . . . .August 15

Exaltation of the Holy Cross. . . . . .September 14

All Saints . . . . .November 1

Christ the King. . . . . .Last Sunday in Ordinary Time

Thanksgiving Day . . . . Fourth Thursday in November

Immaculate Conception . . . . .December 8

March 19 (during Lent)
SAINT JOSEPH

Before the meal

Leader: Blessed are you, God of mercy and wisdom,
for choosing Joseph
to care for the needs of Jesus and Mary,
and for making him the intercessor
for your Church throughout the world.
Though our sins are like scarlet,
they shall be white as snow.

All: Though they are red as crimson,
they shall be made like wool.

Leader: God of our ancestors,
bless the food and drink at our table.
Renew us in mind and body
so we may serve your beloved Son,
Jesus Christ, the Lord.

All: Amen.

After the meal

Leader: Nourishing God,
we thank you for this meal
and for all your gifts to this household.
Show to all people,
especially those who lack enough to eat,
your goodness and loving-kindness in Christ Jesus,
both now and for ever.

All: Amen.

March 19 (when transferred to the Easter Season)
SAINT JOSEPH

Before the meal

Leader: Blessed are you, God of mercy and wisdom,
for choosing Joseph
to care for the needs of Jesus and Mary,
and for making him the intercessor
for those redeemed by Jesus Christ.
For behold, Jesus died
and now lives for evermore. Alleluia!

All: He has gone before us.
Yet he is with us for all time. Alleluia!

Leader: God of our ancestors,
bless the food and drink at our table.
Renew us in mind and body
so we may serve your risen Son,
Jesus Christ, the Lord.

All: Amen.

After the meal

Leader: Nourishing God,
we thank you for this meal
and for all your gifts to this household.
Show to all people,
especially those who lack enough to eat,
your goodness and loving-kindness in Christ Jesus,
both now and for ever.

All: Amen.

March 21 (during Lent)
PASSING OF SAINT BENEDICT, FATHER OF MONKS

Before the meal

Leader: My brothers and sisters,
if we wish to reach eternal life,
we must run and do now
what will profit us for eternity.
Let us return to the Lord, our God.
Though our sins are like scarlet,
they shall be white as snow.

All: Though they are red as crimson,
they shall be made like wool.

Leader: Giver of all good gifts,
bless the food and drink
at this festive meal.
Let it nourish us
on the way to our heavenly homeland,
where Saint Benedict
celebrates life with you and all the saints,
for ever and ever.

All: Amen.

After the meal

Leader: Ever-faithful God,
we thank you for the sacred food
that strengthened Saint Benedict
as he passed over into glory,
and for the welcome nourishment
that we have shared on his solemnity.
Grant us a place with him
at your banquet in heaven,
through Jesus Christ, our Lord.

All: Amen.

March 21 (when transferred to the Easter Season)
PASSING OF SAINT BENEDICT, FATHER OF MONKS

Before the meal

Leader: My brothers and sisters,
if we wish to reach eternal life,
we must run and do now
what will profit us for eternity.
Let us trust in the Lord, our God.
For behold, Jesus died
and now lives for evermore. Alleluia!

All: He has gone before us.
Yet he is with us for all time. Alleluia!

Leader: Giver of all good gifts,
bless the food and drink
at this festive meal.
Let it nourish us
on the way to our heavenly homeland,
where Saint Benedict
celebrates life with you and all the saints,
for ever and ever.

All: Amen.

After the meal

Leader: Ever-faithful God,
we thank you for the sacred food
that strengthened Saint Benedict
as he passed over into glory,
and for the welcome nourishment
that we have shared on his solemnity.
Grant us a place with him
at your paschal feast in heaven,
through Jesus Christ, our Lord.

All: Amen.

March 25 (during Lent)
ANNUNCIATION OF THE LORD

Before the meal

Leader: Blest are you, God of the ages,
for announcing your saving plan in Christ
to the Blessed Virgin Mary.
Our hearts find joy in her Son,
the Word made flesh.
Though our sins are like scarlet,
they shall be white as snow.

All: Though they are red as crimson,
they shall be made like wool.

Leader: God Most High,
send your blessing upon our table
and upon those who prepared this food
for our enjoyment: *(name them).*
We ask this in the name of our Savior,
Jesus Christ, our Lord.

All: Amen.

After the meal

Leader: All-holy God,
you have shared your Son's great dignity with us
in his incarnation, passion, and resurrection.
Receive our thanks for this meal,
and make us mindful
of the needs of the poor and hungry.
With holy Mary, we praise and glorify you,
both now and for ever.

All: Amen.

March 25 (when transferred to the Easter Season)
ANNUNCIATION OF THE LORD

Before the meal

Leader: Blest are you, God of the ages,
for announcing your saving plan in Christ
to the Blessed Virgin Mary.
Our hearts find joy in her Son,
the King of glory.
Behold, Jesus died
and now lives for evermore. Alleluia!

All: He has gone before us.
Yet he is with us for all time. Alleluia!

Leader: God Most High,
send your blessing upon our table
and upon those who prepared this food
for our enjoyment *(name them)*.
We ask this in the name of our risen Savior,
Jesus Christ, our Lord.

All: Amen.

After the meal

Leader: All-holy God,
you have shared your Son's great dignity with us
in his incarnation, passion, and resurrection.
Receive our thanks for this meal,
and make us mindful
of the needs of the poor and hungry.
With holy Mary, we praise and glorify you,
both now and for ever.

All: Amen.

Sunday after Pentecost
MOST HOLY TRINITY

Before the meal

Leader: Blest is our God,
creator and ruler of all things,
the holy and undivided Trinity.
Through God's wisdom and power
we receive all goodness, kindness, and loving favor.

All: Give thanks to the Lord, for he is good,
for his mercy endures for ever.

Leader: God of glory and majesty,
send your blessing upon this food.
May it help us to serve you in love
according to your gracious will,
both now and for ever.

All: Amen.

After the meal

Leader: Lord God,
how wonderful is your kindness to us
in the meal that we have shared.
All praise and honor be yours,
One God in Three Persons,
for ever and ever.

All: Amen.

Sunday after Trinity Sunday
MOST HOLY BODY AND BLOOD OF CHRIST

Before the meal

Leader: Sacred is the eucharistic feast,
the remembrance of all God's marvels
in Christ the Lord.
He sustains us in every hunger
with his goodness, kindness, and loving favor.

All: Give thanks to the Lord, for he is good,
for his mercy endures for ever.

Leader: Nourishing God,
bless the food and drink at this table.
May your generosity to us here
make us generous servants of each other
in the Body of your Son,
Jesus Christ, the Lord.

All: Amen.

After the meal

Leader: Lord Jesus,
we taste your goodness
in the gift of your Body and Blood,
and in the food we have shared at this table.
Bring us one day to your banquet in heaven,
there to savor your merciful love,
for ever and ever.

All: Amen.

Friday after the Body and Blood of Christ
MOST SACRED HEART OF JESUS

Before the meal

Leader: Beyond the mind's knowing
is the marvel we celebrate:
all the love of our God
abides in the human heart of Christ the Lord.
From this fountain of life
we receive his goodness, kindness, and loving favor.

All: Give thanks to the Lord, for he is good,
for his mercy endures for ever.

Leader: Lord Jesus, in your tender love
bestow your blessing on this table
and on all dear to us.
Be for us and for all people
our life and our resurrection,
for ever and ever.

All: Amen.

After the meal

Leader: Lord Jesus, most worthy of all praise,
receive our thanks for the blessings
we have received at this meal.
We place our hope in you, our Savior,
both now and for ever.

All: Amen.

June 24
NATIVITY OF JOHN THE BAPTIST

Before the meal

Leader: Praise be to God for John the Baptist,
last and greatest of the prophets
and forerunner of Christ the Lord.
John prepared the way before the Son of God
so that all people might receive
the Father's goodness, kindness, and loving favor.

All: Give thanks to the Lord, for he is good,
for his mercy endures for ever.

Leader: Lord God,
send your blessing upon this table,
so that in receiving new strength from your gifts,
we may glorify your holy name,
both now and for ever.

All: Amen.

After the meal

Leader: Thanksgiving be yours, O God, for this meal
by which we honor
the glorious birth of John the Baptist.
Let us feast with him
at the table in your kingdom,
for ever and ever.

All: Amen.

Before the meal

Leader: Praise be to God for Saint Peter and Saint Paul:
two teachers of divine wisdom,
two preachers of the Gospel of Christ.
In them we know
his goodness, kindness, and loving favor.

All: Give thanks to the Lord, for he is good,
for his mercy endures for ever.

Leader: We praise you, O God,
as we keep this festival.
Bless our food and drink,
that through this nourishment
we may persevere faithfully
in serving your beloved Son,
Jesus Christ, the Lord.

All: Amen.

After the meal

Leader: We thank you, God of apostles,
for guiding the church built on their faith
and for sustaining this family in your love.
Receive our thanksgiving for this meal
and for all your gifts,
through Jesus Christ, our Lord.

All: Amen.

July 11
BENEDICT,
PATRIARCH OF WESTERN MONASTICISM

Before the meal

Leader: My brothers and sisters,
let us prefer nothing whatever to Christ,
for there is nothing in all creation
that can separate us from the love of God
in Christ Jesus the Lord.
Through him we receive
God's goodness, kindness, and loving favor.

All: Give thanks to the Lord, for he is good,
for his mercy endures for ever.

Leader: Giver of all good gifts,
bless the food and drink at this festive meal,
and make it a source of abundant life and health for us.
As we honor Saint Benedict,
we place our hope in your mercy,
both now and for ever.

All: Amen.

After the meal

Leader: We bless your holy name, ever-faithful God,
as we celebrate the memory of Saint Benedict.
Receive our thanks for the nourishing gifts
that we have joyfully shared as your household,
through Jesus Christ, our Lord.

All: Amen.

ASSUMPTION OF THE BLESSED VIRGIN MARY

Before the meal

Leader: How great is the marvel we celebrate:
Mary has been carried from earth to heaven!
The angels give joyful praise to the Son of God,
who brings us the Father's
goodness, kindness, and loving favor.

All: Give thanks to the Lord, for he is good,
for his mercy endures for ever.

Leader: Mary's God and our God,
grant your blessing to this food and drink,
which we receive from your bounty,
through Jesus Christ, our Lord.

All: Amen.

After the meal

Leader: Gracious God,
as we thank you for your many gifts,
make us mindful of the poor and the hungry.
Let this meal sustain us
on the way to our heavenly homeland,
there to join the Blessed Virgin Mary
and all the saints,
for ever and ever.

All: Amen.

September 14
EXALTATION OF THE HOLY CROSS

Before the meal

Leader: Lover of the world and its peoples,
for our sake
your Son became obedient unto death,
even to death on a cross.
Great are your wonders,
God here among us,
God, our gladness.

All: Let the peoples praise you, O God;
let all the peoples praise you.

Leader: God of mercy,
it is right that we should glory in the cross,
for you bring us life, salvation, and resurrection.
Bestow your blessing upon the food
we are about to share.
Let it nourish us to praise and serve the true King,
Jesus Christ, the Lord.

All: Amen.

After the meal

Leader: Praise to you, Giver of all good gifts,
for by his dying and rising
our Lord Jesus Christ has given us
the life that never ends.
May his holy cross
be the sign of your unfailing protection in our lives,
both now and for ever.

All: Amen.

Before the meal

Leader: We rejoice in you, O Lord,
celebrating a festival day
in honor of all the saints.
At their solemnity the angels rejoice
and give praise to the Son of God.
With the whole company of heaven we proclaim:
Great are your wonders,
God here among us,
God, our gladness.

All: Let the peoples praise you, O God;
let all the peoples praise you.

Leader: Most-holy God,
by the prayerful intercession of your saints,
may your blessing descend upon this meal
and upon those who share it.
Transform us and all creation for your glory,
both now and for ever.

All: Amen.

After the meal

Leader: We thank you, Giver of blessedness,
for the fruits of our earthly harvest,
and we look to that glorious day
when the harvest of your holy ones
will be complete.
Bring us to the table you have prepared
for all who love and serve your Son, Jesus Christ,
who is Lord for ever and ever.

All: Amen.

Last Sunday in Ordinary Time
CHRIST THE KING

Before the meal

Leader: We give you glory, Lord Jesus Christ,
for you reign as King of kings and Lord of lords.
Great are your wonders,
God here among us,
God, our gladness.

All: Let the peoples praise you, O God;
let all the peoples praise you.

Leader: Eternal King,
bestow your blessing upon this table
as you blessed many times
the table of your friends and disciples.
Let these gifts strengthen us in your service,
both now and for ever.

All: Amen.

After the meal

Leader: Thanks be to you, crucified yet risen Savior,
for the abundance you give us here on earth.
Make us share one day
in the joy of the heavenly banquet in your kingdom,
where you are Lord, for ever and ever.

All: Amen.

THANKSGIVING DAY

Before the meal

Leader: The earth has yielded its fruit,
for you, our God, have blessed us generously.
Abundance flows in your steps,
your open hand fills all our needs.
Great are your wonders,
God here among us,
God, our gladness.

All: Let the peoples praise you, O God;
let all the peoples praise you.

Leader: Glory and praise to you, Lord,
for giving us a desirable, good, and ample land;
for making a covenant with us
in your Son, Jesus;
and for granting us life, grace, mercy, and food
in every season.
Bless this festive meal
and this time to enjoy it,
through Jesus Christ, our Lord.

All: Amen.

After the meal

Leader: Generous God,
we give you thanks for the fruits of the earth
and for the labors of those who bring them to our table.
Continue to nourish us and all people
with your steadfast love,
which endures for ever and ever.

All: Amen.

December 8
IMMACULATE CONCEPTION

Before the meal

Leader: Let us glorify God
for the immaculate conception of holy Mary,
from whom came forth Christ the Lord,
the Savior of Eve's children.
Before us a voice cries out:
"Prepare in the wilderness a way for the Lord.
Clear a highway across the desert for our God."

All: Every valley shall be lifted up,
every mountain and hill brought low.

Leader: God of the lowly,
send your blessing upon our table
and upon those who have prepared this food for us.
Make us mindful of the poor and the hungry,
those who are dearest to Mary's Son,
Jesus Christ, the Lord.

All: Amen.

After the meal

Leader: Mary's God and our God,
we thank you for nourishing body and spirit
and for filling the hungry with good things.
Look upon us with favor these Advent days,
and help us to proclaim your greatness,
both now and for ever.

All: Amen.